Ten Po
from the ~~Coast~~

ex libris

Candlestick Press

Published by:

Candlestick Press,
Diversity House, 72 Nottingham Road, Arnold, Nottingham NG5 6LF
www.candlestickpress.co.uk

Design and typesetting by Craig Twigg

Printed by Ratcliff & Roper Print Group, Nottinghamshire, UK

Selection and Introduction © Miriam Darlington, 2022

Cover illustration © Sam Cannon, 2022
www.samcannonart.co.uk

Candlestick Press monogram © Barbara Shaw, 2008

Donation to Surfers Against Sewage
www.sas.org.uk

ISBN 978 1 907598 94 4

Acknowledgements

The poems in this pamphlet are reprinted from the following books, all by
permission of the publishers listed unless stated otherwise. Every effort has been
made to trace the copyright holders of the poems published in this book. The
editor and publisher apologise if any material has been included without
permission or without the appropriate acknowledgement, and would be glad to be
told of anyone who has not been consulted.

Thanks are due to all the copyright holders cited below for their kind permission:

Miriam Darlington, poem first published in this anthology. Helen Dunmore,
Counting Backwards: Poems 1975-2017 (Bloodaxe Books, 2019)
www.bloodaxebooks.com. Jen Hadfield, *Nigh-No-Place* (Bloodaxe Books, 2008)
www.bloodaxebooks.com. Kathleen Jamie, *Love poet, carpenter: Michael
Longley at Seventy*, edited by Robin Robertson (Enitharmon Press, 2009) by kind
permission of the author. Blake Morrison, *Shingle Street* (Chatto and Windus,
2015) by permission of Penguin Random House UK. Kenneth Steven, *Salt and
Light* (St. Andrew Press, 2007) © Kenneth Steven 2007. Used by permission.
Rights@hymnsam.co.uk. Anne Stevenson, *Collected Poems* (Bloodaxe Books,
2023) www.bloodaxebooks.com. Derek Walcott, *Collected Poems 1948-1984*
(Faber & Faber; FSG, 1992). Giles Watson, poem first published in this
anthology.

All permissions cleared courtesy of Suzanne Fairless-Aitken
c/o Swift Permissions swiftpermissions@gmail.com

Where poets are no longer living, their dates are given.

Introduction

For the last twenty years I have lived near the south west coast of England. I can see the sun rise over the hill to the east and watch it set over the hill to the west. From the south the air comes charged with the tang of Atlantic weather and seaweed. In between, water-worn pebbles, sand and rock crinkle into tidal reaches and estuary. Salty suspensions breathe into reedy marshes and town edges, playing with the human landscape and the tide's first bridging point.

The poems here express some of the elemental nature of archipelagic nations, in all their wonder and diversity. We are joined to the aquatic ecosystem yet do not always pay attention to it. Years ago, I lived on a tiny island in the Atlantic, where contact with coastal weather, moon and tide was always vividly present. Now the cycles are so engrained in me that sometimes I see the valley in front of my suburban house fill up with seawater and empty again, washing the air clean as if a ghost-tide were there. For all of us living on this watery planet, this shadowy dynamism is never far from our consciousness.

To come to the coast is not just to recharge ourselves with the joys of oxygen and serotonin but to see ourselves anew, in a meditative context, where ecological protection and challenge are ever present. To be next to the water is to be more deeply human in the world. To be, as Giles Watson says "at our most alien and most delighted".

The coast can be "a wrecking ground," as in Blake Morrison's 'Shingle Street'; a place to think, with Matthew Arnold, about how humanity is "swept with confused alarms of struggle and flight, / where ignorant armies clash by night" or a place to be soothed by "the amen of calm waters", for Derek Walcott in his prayerful and propitious 'Sea-Chantey'.

Moods and weather patterns are brought into sharp relief and intersect with perfect synergy here. Looking out into the blue expanse we see reflected the bubbling turbulence of our inner lives, as well as that of our non-human kin, and are compelled to capture them in the best words we can, for others to feel.

Interconnectedness enters us through the senses in a poem. Leaving or arriving, collecting, or shedding, both the sensorium and creativity are enlivened on beach, seawall, harbour or cliff: "I go to the rockpool at the slack of the tide / to mind me what my poetry's for," says Jen Hadfield, making an imaginative connection between the possibilities of water and the page, and between body and spirit.

In these poems we encounter an enhanced surround-sound of elementals: the crumble of a cliff edge, the scent of the tidal seabed, bursts of fresh salt spray. These poems from the coast enfold animal, mineral, vegetable and soul. It's a dreaming place, to wonder: who am I? What is myth and what is real? What do I long for? What are we doing?

Here at the water's edge we are brought into the realm of quest and possibility, and all that entails for the self, and for finding our place in the world. The coast has always been a place of transition: grief and transience; hope and despair. The windy soundscape of seabirds throws us a mix of scream and serenade, at once soothing and unsettling.

Uniquely, the edges of land and sea are where we can properly sense safety in the landscape of home, calling to us like a song we have long missed. It is joyful and yet reminds us of losses: our own primal amniotic bliss, closeness to loved ones; tragedy and conflicts; voyages, adventure, piracy, even lunacy. We fear and cherish the coast for all this, for better or for worse.

All these human things are cast upon the sea without the sea ever having asked for any of it. All around the planet a riptide of emotion settles on coastlines.

Leavings, arrivals, births and drownings. Land slips away, land reshapes itself. How very small we are, and how tiny our habitable part of the earth, all so fragile and yet robust amongst the ever-dynamic workings of words, water and climate.

Miriam Darlington

Iona Ferry

It's the smell I remember –
The dizziness of diesel, tarry rope, wood sheened like toffee.
The sea was waving in the wind, a dancing –
I wanted it to be rough and yet I didn't.
My mother and I snugged under the awning,
To a dark rocking. We were as low as the waves,
All of us packed in tight like bales of wool.

The engine roared alive, its tremor
Juddered through the wood and thrilled me, beat my heart.
The shore began fading behind the white curl of our hum.
Fourteen days lay barefoot on the island –
Still asleep, their eyes all shut.
And yet I knew them all already,
Felt them in my pocket like polished stones –
Their orchids, their hurt-white sand, their larksong.

Kenneth Steven

Cliffs of Fall

(to the memory of Gerard Manley Hopkins)

Spring of turf and thrift, tangle of fleece, sheep-shit,
Subtle flowers where honeybees knock
At the foxglove lip and the gorse trap

Then sheer on our left the drop. Spatter of bracken hooks
Misleading the lambs. In the bank, marsh violets
Wet, lovely, minute. We need not look for the fall, the chink

Of pebble that tumbles. All the grey scree stirs
Slip-rattles and stills itself. Here is the slope's
Angle, implacable. Here's where you look

Touch, unbalance, dislodge. Infinite drop
Where the bee burrs at the foxglove's lip,
All quick-tongued, intimate.

Time to step back to the wide margin
Cleave to the path's dapper attention
Unspring each poem,

Pitch each new note to the key of loss,
Lose nothing. Stay clear of the drop
Where the world bursts through its dirty glass.

Sun on your neck, a dazzle of violets
Infinitely slipsliding –
No quick wing-beat of flight, but a slope

Of gravel-rubble, its angle implacable
Stripping you raw. From here your fall
Is a matter of form: a slow marvel.

Helen Dunmore (1952 – 2017)

Daed-traa

I go to the rockpool at the slack of the tide
to mind me what my poetry's for.

It has ventricles, just like us –
pumping brine, like bull's blood, a syrupy flow.

It has its theatre –
hushed and plush.

It has its Little Shop of Horrors.
It has its crossed and dotted monsters.

It has its cross-eyed beetling Lear.
It has its billowing Monroe.

I go to the rockpool at the slack of the tide
to mind me what my poetry's for.

For monks, it has barnacles
to sweep the broth as it flows, with fans,
grooming every cubic millimetre.

It has its ebb, the easy heft of wrack from rock,
like plastered, feverish locks of hair.

It has its *flodd*.
It has its welling god
with puddled, podgy cheeks and jaw.

It has its holy hiccup.

Its minute's silence

daed-traa.

I go to the rockpool at the slack of the tide
to mind me what my poetry's for.

Jen Hadfield

Dover Beach

The sea is calm tonight.
The tide is full, the moon lies fair
Upon the straits; on the French coast the light
Gleams and is gone; the cliffs of England stand,
Glimmering and vast, out in the tranquil bay.
Come to the window, sweet is the night-air!
Only, from the long line of spray
Where the sea meets the moon-blanched land,
Listen! you hear the grating roar
Of pebbles which the waves draw back, and fling,
At their return, up the high strand,
Begin, and cease, and then again begin,
With tremulous cadence slow, and bring
The eternal note of sadness in.

Sophocles long ago
Heard it on the Aegean, and it brought
Into his mind the turbid ebb and flow
Of human misery; we
Find also in the sound a thought,
Hearing it by this distant northern sea.

The Sea of Faith
Was once, too, at the full, and round earth's shore
Lay like the folds of a bright girdle furled.
But now I only hear
Its melancholy, long, withdrawing roar,
Retreating, to the breath
Of the night-wind, down the vast edges drear
And naked shingles of the world.

Ah, love, let us be true
To one another! for the world, which seems
To lie before us like a land of dreams,
So various, so beautiful, so new,
Hath really neither joy, nor love, nor light,

Nor certitude, nor peace, nor help for pain;
And we are here as on a darkling plain
Swept with confused alarms of struggle and flight,
Where ignorant armies clash by night.

Matthew Arnold (1822 – 1888)

North Sea off Carnoustie

You know it by the northern look of the shore,
by salt-worried faces,
an absence of trees, an abundance of lighthouses.
It's a serious ocean.

Along marram-scarred, sandbitten margins
wired roofs straggle out to where
a cold little holiday fair
has floated in and pitched itself
safely near the prairie of a golf course.
Coloured lights have sunk deep into the solid wind,
but all they've caught is a pair of lovers
and three silly boys.
Everyone else has a dog.
Or a room to get to.

The smells are of fish and of sewage and cut grass.
Oystercatchers, doubtful of habitation,
clamour *weep, weep, weep*, as they fuss over
scummy black rocks the tide leaves for them.

The sea is as near as we come to another world.

But there in your stony and windswept garden
a blackbird is confirming the grip of the land.
You, you, he murmurs, dark purple in his voice.

And now in far quarters of the horizon
lighthouses are awake, sending messages –
invitations to the landlocked,
warnings to the experienced,
but to anyone returning from the planet ocean,
candles in the windows of a safe earth.

Anne Stevenson (1933 – 2020)

Beyond the Lighthouses

I think of them soaring past Skerryvore:
gannets, fulmars, over the green-gold machair,
their switch-back wave-skip round Bishop and Wolf,
sailing by Shipman's Head or Staffa, to Unst, Bempton.
Cresting the spume, scudding above sea-caves and cliffs,
with the kittiwakes and razorbills; keepers of unnamed places,
dropping to the foam like silver beads, in a milky way of fish-scale,
oil-bellied darlings of the wind. The lights sweep them a saffron spray
on skerries and skelligs, all the way from Bass Rock to St. Kilda,
where they meet to settle their fleeting faith in this land,
its rock-ledges, sea beet and thrift. Snowy breast
on snowy breast – nearly but not quite ours –
they bow and nod to their own heart's-fit,
to the plump gift of a mate or an egg,
safe in the clasp of the wind.

Miriam Darlington

A Sea-Chantey

Là, tout n'est qu'ordre et beauté,
Luxe, calme et volupté.
- Baudelaire

Anguilla, Adina,
Antigua, Cannelles,
Andreuille, all the *l's*,
Voyelles, of the liquid Antilles,
The names tremble like needles
Of anchored frigates,
Yachts tranquil as lilies,
In ports of calm coral,
The lithe, ebony hulls
Of strait-stitching schooners,
The needles of their masts
That thread archipelagoes
Refracted embroidery
In feverish waters
Of the seafarer's islands,
Their shorn, leaning palms,
Shaft of Odysseus,
Cyclopic volcanoes,
Creak their own histories,
In the peace of green anchorage;
Flight, and Phyllis,
Returned from the Grenadines,
Names entered this Sabbath,
In the port clerk's register;
Their baptismal names,
The sea's liquid letters,
Repos donnez à cils...
And their blazing cargoes
Of charcoal and oranges;
Quiet, the fury of their ropes.
Daybreak is breaking
On the green chrome water,
The white herons of yachts

Are at Sabbath communion,
The histories of schooners
Are murmured in coral,
Their cargoes of sponges
On sandspits of islets,
Barques white as white salt
Of acrid St. Maarten,
Hulls crusted with barnacles,
Holds foul with great turtles,
Whose ship-boys have seen
The blue heave of Leviathan,
A sea-faring, Christian,
And intrepid people.

Now an apprentice washes his cheeks
With salt water and sunlight.

In the middle of the harbour
A fish breaks the Sabbath
With a silvery leap.
The scales fall from him
In a tinkle of churchbells;
The town streets are orange
With the week-ripened sunlight,
Balanced on the bowsprit
A young sailor is playing
His grandfather's chantey
On a trembling mouth organ;
The music curls, dwindling
Like smoke from blue galleys,
To dissolve near the mountains.
The music uncurls with
The soft vowels of inlets,
The christening of vessels,
The titles of portages,
The colours of sea grapes,

The tartness of sea-almonds,
The alphabet of church bells,
The peace of white horses,
The pastures of ports,
The litany of islands,
The rosary of archipelagoes,
Anguilla, Antigua,
Virgin of Guadeloupe,
And stone-white Grenada
Of sunlight and pigeons,
The amen of calm waters,
The amen of calm waters,
The amen of calm waters.

Derek Walcott (1930 – 2017)

Poem

I walk at the land's edge,
turning in my mind
a private predicament.
Today the sea is indigo.
Thirty years an adult –
same mind, same
ridiculous quandaries –
but every time the sea
appears differently: today
a tumultuous dream,
flinging its waves ashore –

Nothing resolved,
I tread back over the moor
– but every time the moor
appears differently: this evening,
tufts of bog-cotton
unbutton themselves in the wind
– and then comes the road
so wearily familiar
the old shining road
that leads everywhere

Kathleen Jamie

from **The Ballad of Shingle Street**

...On Shingle Street
The shelving's steep
With stones to skim
As if they'd feet
To hop and skip
Across the deep,
To pitter-pat and aquaplane,
Again again again again,
Not flip and flop, and splash and drop,
The opened trap, the hangman's rope,
The cairns that mark where life gave out,
The muddy dark off Shingle Street.

From Shingle Street
To Bawdsey Bay
The sea-mews shriek
Above the spray,
The rolling seals
Are charcoal grey
As though burnt out or singed by grief.
Like ash-streaked mourners, half-possessed,
They duck and bob and stare to land
In hope that we might understand.
But nothing helps, we fail the test,
They hang and gaze without relief
Beyond the reach of Shingle Street.

For Shingle Street's a single street,
A row of shacks in stone and wood,
The sea out front, the marsh out back,
Just one road in and one road out,
With no way north except the spit,
And no way south except on foot,
A cul-de-sac, a dead-end track,
A sandbanked strand to sink a fleet,
A bay, a bar, a strip, a trap,
A wrecking ground, that's Shingle Street.

On Shingle Street
As sunset seeps
Across the marsh
The flocks of kale
Are grazing sheep,
A soft pink light
Sneaks up the beach
As if each stone were ringed with fire,
As if each pebble stored the heat
Of past disasters, past defeats...

Blake Morrison

Estuary

Here, of all places, I am most alien, and most delighted,
where every voice is otherworldly, curlewing into space
wide as mudflats at low tide, and every layer of grey
is a different shade, swathes of polished oystershell. Place
not our place but theirs – plovers light as spindrift, tall
whimbrels shivering the distance, flocks of cloud-dark
knots, turn-billed, stilt-high godwits with their backs
to the wind that brought them – place of distance, ancient
terminus, place of feeding, breeding, flying on, place
of flux and stillness, place which replicates across wide
hemispheres, joined in a bird's eye by lines of instinct,
plumbed by the Earth's magnet. Place where I come
to leave myself, to die to rootedness, to expose my breast
to the wind's cold euphoria. Place to praise, forget – and fly.

Giles Watson